The Art of Transition

Workbook

Sara J. Simons

The Art of Transition Workbook

First published in Great Britain by Springtime Books 2020

Copyright: Sara Simons

ISBN: 978-1-8381746-1-3

THE **WAY** BETWEEN

This workbook would not have come into being without the support of several special people in my life.

A big thanks goes out to...

Buck Rogers, my mentor and coach. You introduced me to life-planning and believed I had something new to contribute. Thank you for continually challenging me to to live the material through my own transitions while setting "shipping dates" all along the way.

Thank you to Sandee Hunt, my very creative friend who inspired me to "draw near," when I really was very scared and shy with my creative expressions. You gave me the courage to print my simple drawings here to hopefully inspire the creative side in others.

To Jeannine Pringle, my graphic designer, for so willingly doing the nitty-gritty details when I didn't really know what I wanted. You were always so teachable and patient. Thank you for making this happen.

To the many cross-cultural workers in transition who let me try out this material on them in the different stages along the way. Thank you for entrusting me with your joys and your pain.

And finally to my wonderful partner and soulmate, Jeff, for letting me brainstorm out loud. Thank you for believing that I needed to get this creative process out of me. You always encouraged me to dig deeper into the creative artist that God placed inside of me.

Thank you for meeting me in My Way Between.

A CANVAS

What would you do with a canvas,
a brush, and colors?
What could you bring to a table set blank
with paints, and space to make your mark,
to leave your print.

I have a feeling He's given us permission
to pick the paints,
and the colors that reflect us.

I know he's given us a place no one else has.
Has established our borders
to protect what we need to flourish.

Yes, what would you do if you believed,
the colors were yours to choose,
the place yours to claim.

You might just spread up as high as out.
Reach that little bit,
like the Eiffel Tower.

Or you might turn in and write,
words that in their singular state
nudge the world when they connect.

Or you might express
your expansive heart,
with colors wild and free.

And when you look at what you've made
you might hold your breath,
and say, 'This? This, is me?'

So, take your brilliant gift,
dance, and draw,
and create with it.

Because I don't think the table
is set in concrete.
Rather, it's a moveable feast.

And please don't say,
things can never change
when we all hold the canvas and pen.

Ask yourself,
what would you do with a canvas,
a brush, and colors?
Then paint yourself
the colors you'd be.

—Ana Lisa de Jong

Welcome

In the space between acknowledging the losses of the past and embracing the new in one's life, exists a predictably chaotic but incredibly beautiful season to create something new and live more fully into your calling. *The Way Between* was birthed from such a season. As well, it exists to aid in the creation and clarifying process that can emerge from one's messy and confused season of searching and grieving. The content of this workbook is organized into universal re-occurring themes of the transition experience:

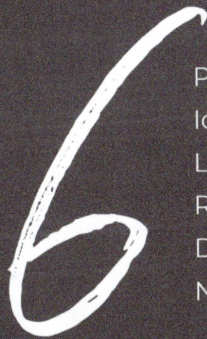

6

Perspective
Identity
Limitations
Reconciliation
Dreams
New Moves

This type of strategic processing is done utilizing both logic and creative brain integration.

TYPES of PROCESSING TOOLS:

I :: Movement techniques for each of the 6 themes to aide you in physical processing

II :: Unstuck Tools are methods to help you in getting unstuck, wherever you are in the journey

III :: Transition Tools for each of the 6 themes to aide you in visual processing

How to use this workbook:

The marriage of movement, art and strategic planning is what makes this material unique. There is an intentionality to the order in which you engage. Starting slowly, almost as a warm up for your brain.

GOAL:
By the end you will have worked from gaining perspective, to exploring identity and limitations, considering where reconciliation is needed, and integrating your dreams into several concrete new moves.

The unstuck tools and movement tools intentionally correspond with each transition theme and coinciding transition tool. This workbook is designed to be a flexible resource if you do choose to skip an exercise. You can come back to it late. There is also space in th back to repeat tools.

MOVEMENT TOOLS

When our body takes on the pain of stress or burnout, it is within our ability to help our bodies release it healthily, developing good coping mechanisms in times of prolonged stress.

One of the best things you can do for yourself is to actively engage the right brain through kinesthetic movement. Give the left, analytical side a much-needed break! When you walk, or draw, or ride a bike, the repetitive physical movements allow your mind a chance for stillness and relief. Your body enters into a more stable place where your mind alone cannot go. It's as if we must let our bodies lead our hearts and minds to calm. Our body can be our best teacher if we learn to listen to it. We can redirect our confused thoughts through simple movements.

UNSTUCK TOOLS

We all experience blocks. The unstuck tools were designed as warm-up exercises prior to self-reflection. They build on one another from one exercise to the next. No one will be judging or grading your skills. Utilize this space to expand on your creativity.

Each unstuck tool and body movement exercise is an invitation to centeredness. Start with the following simple exercise as you begin:

1. Get centered: Focus on your breathing
2. Open up: Be aware of sounds, sensations, and ideas
3. Observe: Watch what comes & goes, internally and externally
4. Try to sway from judgment or interpretation of what you're experiencing

TRANSITION TOOLS

The invitation here is to strategically process holistically. You will be building upon the art and movement exercises you already used, further integrating the right and left brain through creative life-planning tools. You are invited to discover within yourself deeper levels of processing capable through these unique means.

Where to start?
Many of the tools start with a mind-map. Use the gradual progression to expand your thinking.

Then utilizing the examples, design your own visual given the instructions provided. You will discover new ways of seeing and approaching complex decisions.

Let's get started!

KEY

🏃 = Movement/Posture Exercise

⛔ = Getting Unstuck Tool

🚩 = Transition Tool

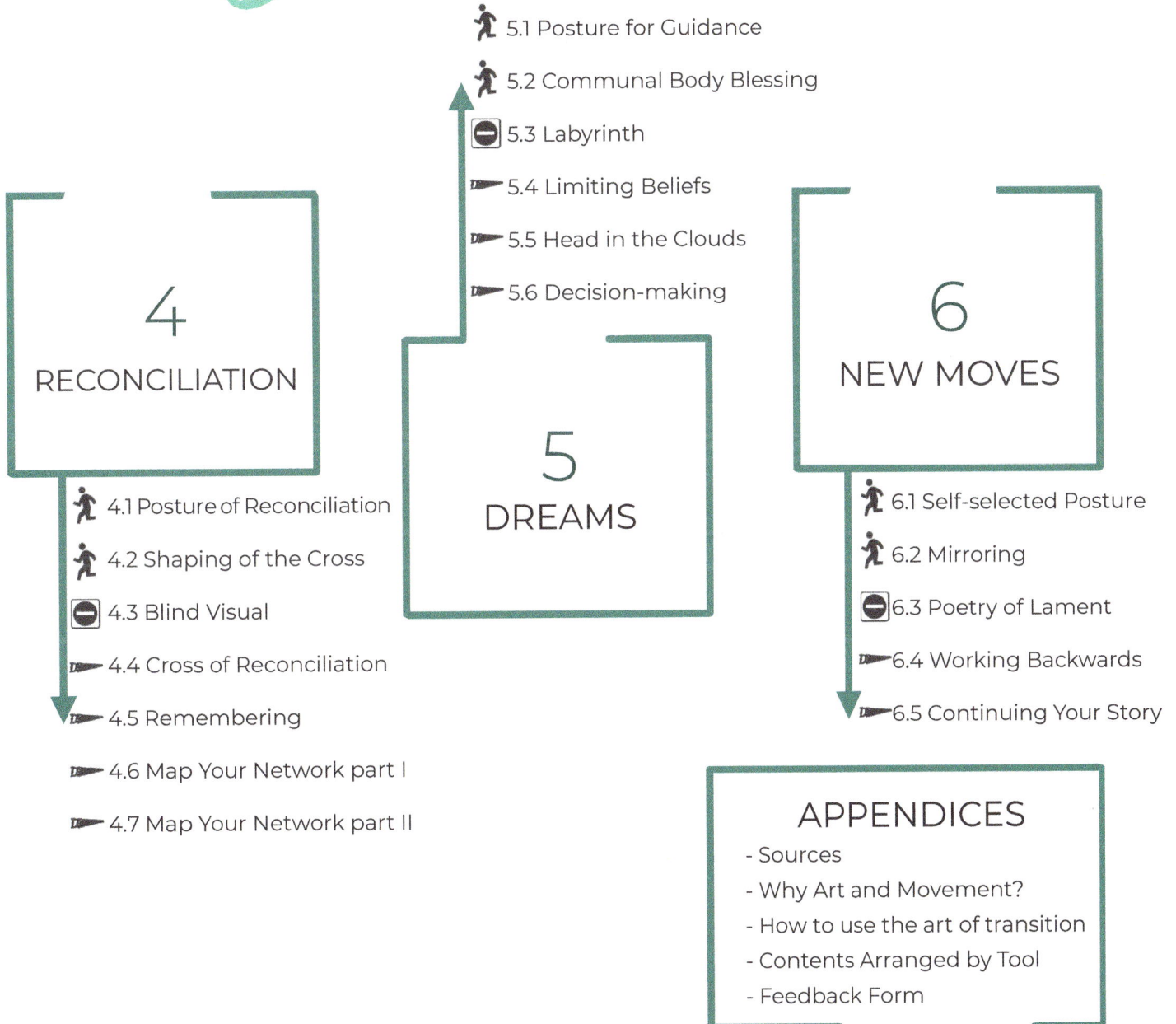

Contents

Transition is a process of grieving the old and
recognizing a need for the new. Some of the greatest shaping in
our lives happens during these
confused times of in-between.

— Terry Walling.

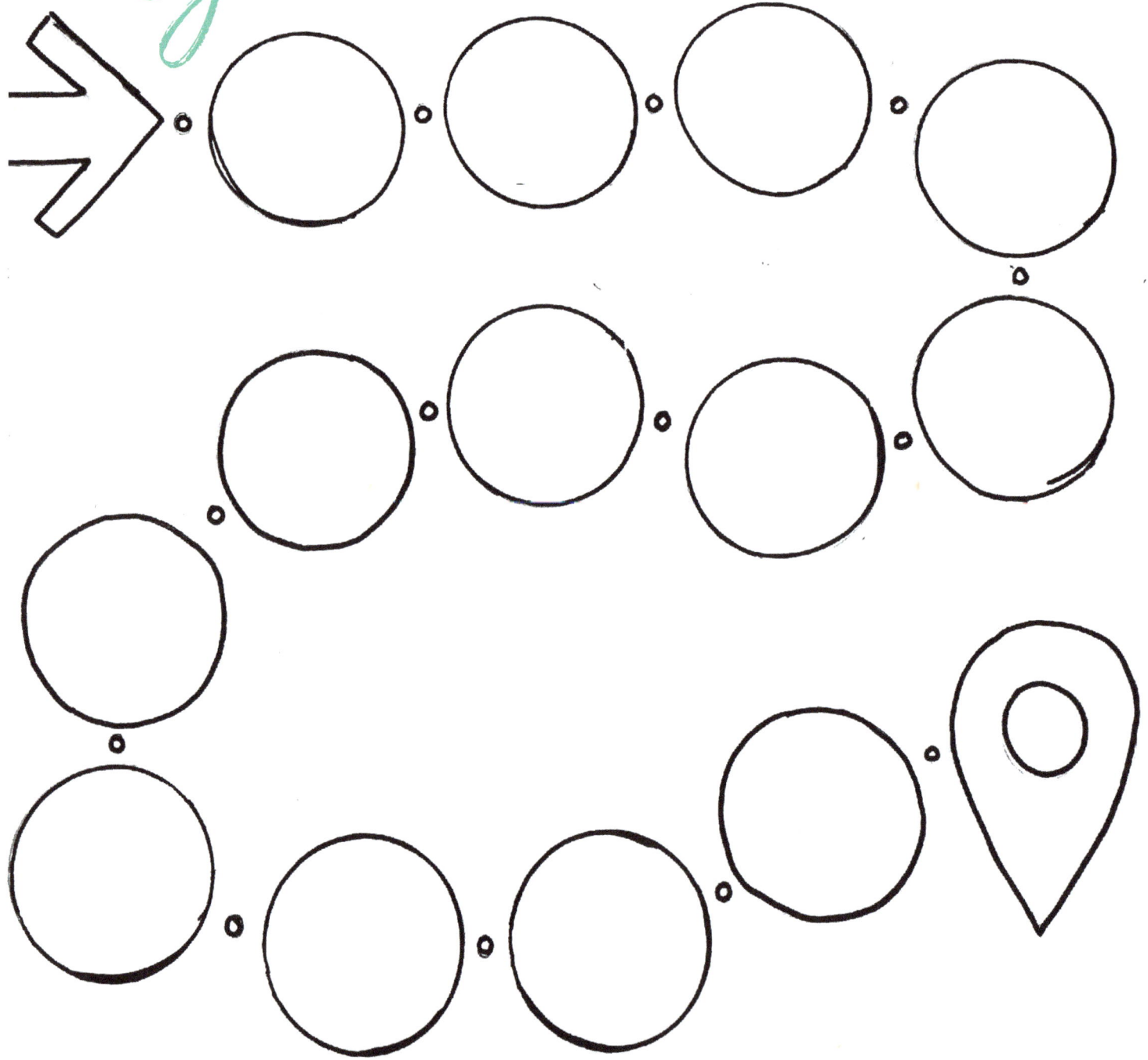

Goldmine

This page is designed as a "gold mine" page for you to consolidate your top one or two take-aways from each exercise. You may choose to cut this out and utilize it as a bookmark as you go along or leave it here, continually coming back to it.

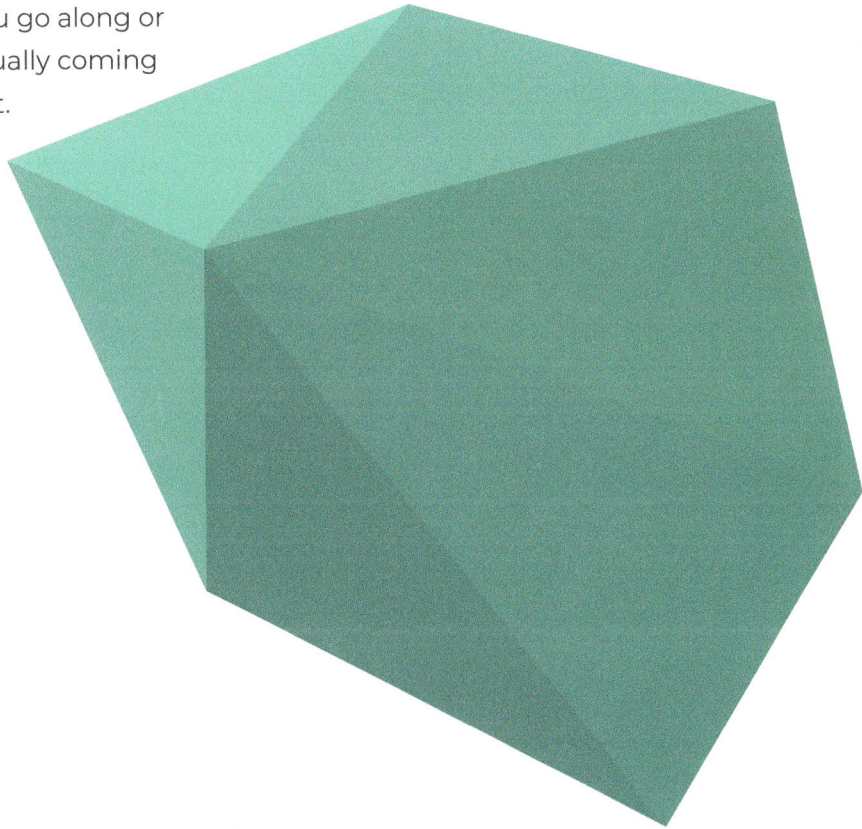

These tabs are to here to help you keep track of where you are within this workbook and mark out each of the the six sections.

PERSPECTIVE

IDENTITY

LIMITATIONS

RECONCILIATION

DREAMS

NEW MOVES

APPENDIX

Perspective

I wait.
I wait for peace.
I wait for what Jesus promised.
I wait in my schedules, in my agendas,
in my life's routine.
I wait and I extend my hope.
To believe
That God will deliver me.
And I will be made new.

– Doug Pagitt

Meditation 8

Centering Meditation

(~5 min)

1. Focus on deep breaths
2. As you breathe in and out,
   be aware of sounds all around you
   and ideas that come to your mind
3. Acknowledge them, but try to sway
   from judgment

Breath Prayer

Breath Prayer

(~5 min)

Focus on deep breaths

Pray while inhaling and exhaling
Father (inhale), thank you (exhale)
Jesus (inhale), thank you (exhale)
Spirit (inhale), thank you (exhale)

(~20 min)

Re-creation

Lift your arms out and up into a "V" position. Reach towards the sky. Reflect on the Creator's ongoing work of re-creation in your life and in the lives of those around you.

Why

We join with all of creation. In this position we wait for new life. We ask for renewed minds and bodies and hearts. We join in the ongoing re-creation process as we ask God to do anew in us what God has done throughout time.

Reflect

How does engaging your body in this way help or hinder you in this process? Journal or draw your reflection.

POSTURE OF
Re-creation

The artist within you speaks to that part of you which yearns for beauty and creativity. Your inner artist invites you to participate in the great work of healing the world by lifting out of your senses, creative images, words, and actions that inspire others to live lives of wonder and surprise.

— Macrina Wiederkehr

Perspective Walk

Perspective Walk

(~30 mins)

Take yourself on a walk! Seek to find a place that provides a different view on life—whether the top of a hill, a street you've never been down, or a rooftop terrace. Ask the Creator to give you a new view on your current circumstances. Contemplate the scene as one of the Creator's masterpieces.

What does the work of the Divine Artist have to teach you about your creativity and the creative process?

PERSPECTIVE

(~ 20 min)

Consider the word at the top of each box. Let your pencil and emotions naturally guide you to express how this word feels to you. Utilize thick or thin lines, scribbles, pressure, shading, and speed as you feel led. Let your hand move at will, expressing the emotion. Avoid using color, recognizable pictures or symbols.

After you finish, take a moment to consider what the visual representations speak to you.

Journal any observations or feelings that come up in the remaining time.

Irritated	Happy
Angry	Peaceful

Shading Exercise

Sad/Depressed	Masculine
Anxious/Worried	Feminine

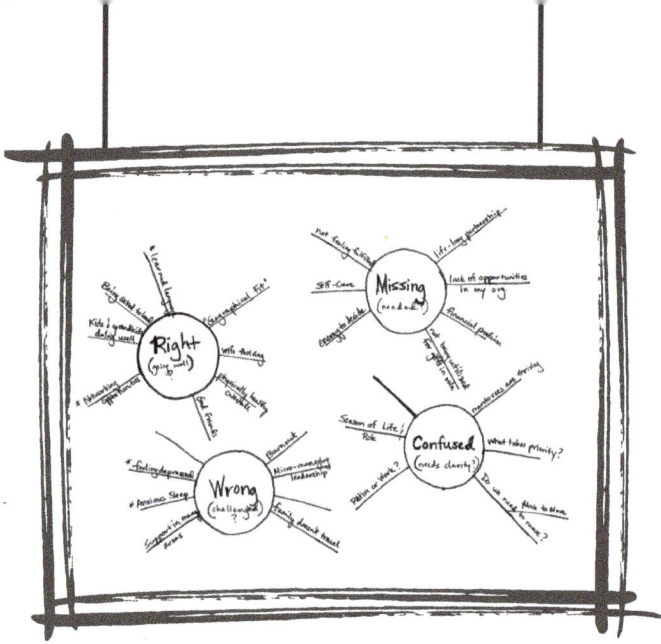

Taking Your Pulse PART I

ART GUIDELINES:

Taking Your Pulse part I

(~30 min)

A Mindmap is a simple visual way to sort, categorize, analyze or make connections between ideas and thoughts. We will be starting most exercises in this book with a Mindmap to get the flow going.

1. Consider these 4 questions: What's right? What's wrong? What's missing? What's confused? About my current situation.
2. Begin by using the blank space to brainstorm and create a mind map around the four questions (see example).
3. Draw 4 circles. Write the words "right", "wrong", "missing", and "confused", in each circle.
4. Branching out from each circle, write words or short phrases that correspond with each word, listing dynamics you are currently experiencing. Feel free to move back and forth in no particular order.

· **What's right? (working well)** Where do you sense God's blessing? Where have you been affirmed?
· **What's wrong? (challenged)** Where are you experiencing greatest struggle? Where do you need to focus greater efforts?
· **What's missing? (needed)** Where is the gap between problems and answers? Where do you need the greatest help?
· **What's confused? (needs clarity)** Where do you feel the most stuck? Where are the pieces not coming together?

COACHING QUESTION:

What is highlighted for you about where you are currently at?

Taking Your Pulse part II

(~30 min)

1. Visualize the journey you are currently on as a game board.
2. Draw a game board of your creative choosing using squares or circles as "spaces".
3. Choose 4 symbols to represent each of the 4 questions from "Taking Your Pulse part I", What's right, wrong, missing, and confused in your current situation.
4. Write a few descriptive words in each square or space to represent your current life.
5. Add color and other twists, turns, bridges, or set-back markers if you like to represent the current dynamics.

COACHING QUESTION:

What are your top 1-2 observations in each category? List your highlights on the "Goldmine" page at the beginning.

Taking Your Pulse
PART II

:: INSPIRATION ::

The Game of Life

The game of Life, also known as just LIFE, is a board game created in 1860 by Milton Bradley. The game simulates a person's journey through his or her life, from birth to college to retirement, with the possibility of jobs, marriage and children all along the way. The object is to land on "good" spaces, to gain small add-on pieces, and to gain extra points by reaching a "happy old age." The base metaphor inspires the idea that life is full of opportunity and can take many different paths. This board game has a narrative and a structure with fictional characters and story lines. But our real journeys are much more unpredictable—some things going right, some confusing, others missing, and some just plain wrong; and still some hold all of the above dynamics! Thinking of life through that ebb and flow allows for a more fluid approach. Additionally, we are not alone in these times of pain and transition.

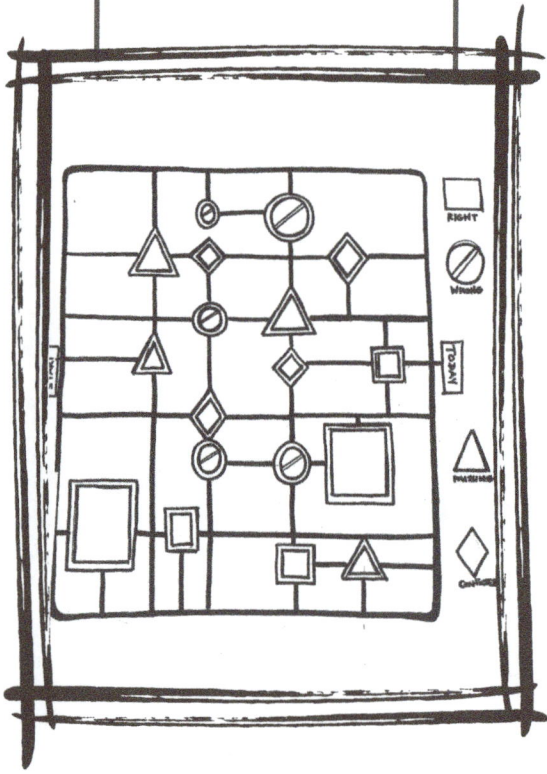

Art enables us to find
ourselves and lose ourselves
at the same time.

— *Thomas Merton*

Unique Wiring part I

(~60 min)

1. There are many things that make you, YOU. Consider the following 3 categories: Natural Abilities, Acquired Skills, and Spiritual Gifts. Make a creative mindmap using some of the key elements of your unique makeup. (See example on the next page).

2. Collect results from inventories that you've taken in the last 5 years – Strengths Finder, Myers Briggs, Grip Birkman, Enneagram, etc. Add these to your mindmap under Natural Abilities/Personality.

3. Expand beyond the words given in the inventories to more fully describe you, like using a thesaurus. List these out as you go.

Examples: Natural abilities: Empathy, teaching, ideation, analytical; Acquired skills: Organization, facilitating, language-learning; Spiritual gifts: Exhortation, leadership, teaching.

COACHING QUESTION:

What from your findings surprises you? Which of your unique "wired" elements are you currently engaged in? What part of your unique wiring are you not utilizing, or is hidden in this season?

Unique Wiring
PART I

:: INSPIRATION ::

Most everyone is familiar with the words of the psalmist: "For you created my inmost being; you knit me together in my mother's womb. I praise you because I am fearfully and wonderfully made..." (Psalm 139). What are some of the tangible signs of this personalized and unique work in each of us? Spiritual gifts are one of the forms we often think of those powerfully and mysteriously imparted spiritual workings that we are given to both discover, practice and mature in as part of our Kingdom participation. However amazing these gifts from the Spirit are, they are only a slice of the larger picture of who God has created us to be! J. Robert Clinton provides a helpful framework in describing a leader's "giftedness set"— the overlapping integration of our 1. Spiritual Gifts; 2. Natural Abilities 3. Acquired Skills. These are all signs of how we are uniquely knit together. In this exercise, we take inventory of some broader categories to get a more holistic grasp of our best knowledge of our unique wiring.

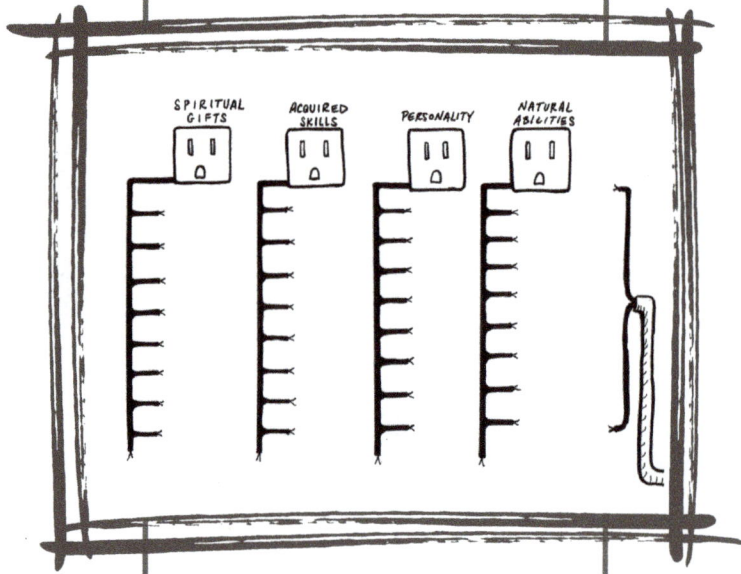

There are beginnings
and endings all the way along the path.
You are constantly letting go
of who you thought you were
and how you thought life would be.

— William Bridges

Unique Wiring
PART II

Unique Wiring part II

(~45 min)

1. Using a colored pencil, circle or draw a line connecting "like" elements across your lists (e.g. teaching as a gift from God, facilitating as an acquired skill, teaching as a natural ability).

2. Now create a way to represent the largest 3 overlapping categories as seen on the previous page with the heart illustration. Make sure each word or phrase is represented or listed on your drawing.

3. The overlap of these three dimensions creates a "sweet spot". This is place where a person is able to make a significant impact and is energized while doing it. This is who you *are* no matter what you *do*.

4. Bonus: Write a sweet spot statement in the space provided. You may choose to do it two ways:

   A. Play with a combination of the top words you use to describe yourself. Make 3 pairs from the words listed in the overlap section. (i.e. Resourcing Developer, or Creative Catalyst)

   B. Fill in the blanks with your sweet spot words. "When I do _____, _____, and _____, others experience ____, _____, or _____" (i.e. When I innovate, facilitate and lead, others experience freedom, are released to imagine and develop their best life.)

Identity

I only know Divine unconditional, radical and reckless love for me when I dare to approach God just as I am.

— David Benner

POSTURE FOR
Rest

(~20 min)

Rest
Read Doug Pagitt's poem on the next page. Then, while laying in a comfortable rest position, with hands facing up, meditate on what you have just read and the truth of your identity in Christ.
Feel free to meditate as long as you desire.

Why
It is hard but necessary to create a safe space of silence and rest. A posture of surrender reminds us that we are not in charge; the Creator is. He wants us to join Him in the plans He has for our life.

Reflect
How does this posture feel to you?

I've been thinkin'
About a dream.
I hope you'll join me,
where forming means
Are unfolding and it seems
to me…
That you've been thinkin'
About a dream.
and you've got a reason
To believe
And I'm hoping that we see…
That we've arrived by fountain
Been pursued through the sky.
And in times of renouncement
What was dead is on the rise.
If those who stood beneath Him

Heard Him breathe.
And suppose we had only
Heard Him scream, "It is finished."
So it seemed, But He…
Givin' faith to my dreams
And death has lost its sting.
My life will ever be awakened.
And when from death I'm free
I will sing on
Wholly reconciled.
And when from death we're free
we will sing on
and through eternity we will sing on.

— Doug Pagitt

Body Listening

Body Listening

(~20 min)

Center: Focus on your breathing.

Open up: Be aware of sounds, sensations, ideas.

Observe: Watch what comes & goes.

Sway from judgment or interpretation.

Pay attention to how each part of your body feels. Start from your feet and work your way up through your body.

Silently ask one question at a time and then listen...

What is my body trying to teach me today?

What questions is my body asking?

Present a prayer of gratitude for what has been revealed.

Journal or draw your reflection.

*Note: You can also do this exercise while walking

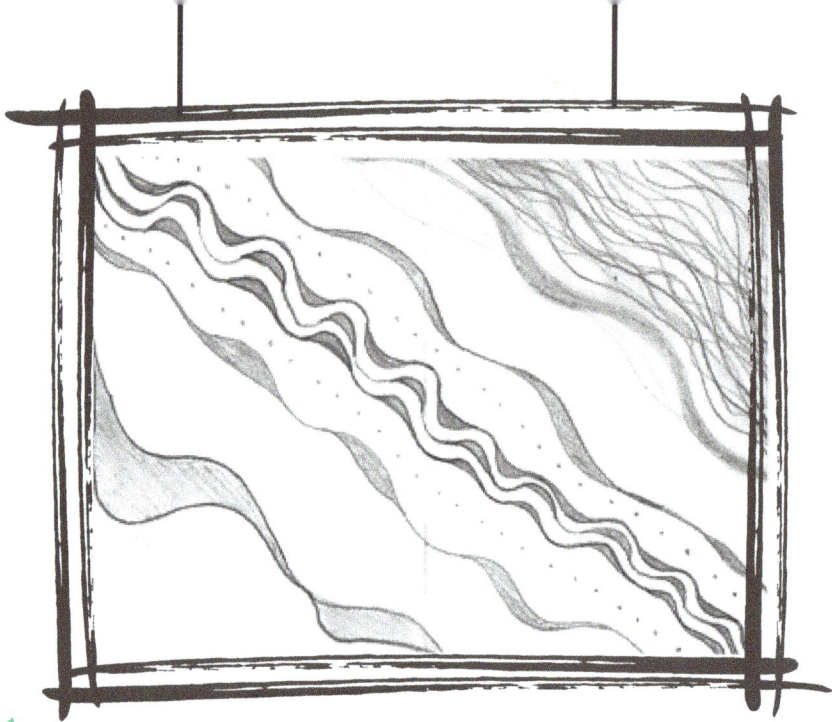

Stuck! free-draw

Stuck! Free-draw

(~20 min)

Center Yourself: Relax and take a few deep, slow breaths. Focus on listening to your breathing and how your body is feeling.

Invite the Creator to fill you with peace and guide you as you think about an area where you are stuck.

Set a timer for 15-20 minutes.

Draw a frame to help you contain and focus, draw a frame on your paper to draw within. It can be any shape of frame. You will be making an abstract, free-form drawing.

• Just get started by moving your pencil and drawing with hunches, feelings, and slowly explore your way through. It is kind of like drawing a cloud — a bit unclear and not exact. It may come in bits and spurts.

• Feel free to stop when you feel you have expressed enough. Journal any observations here.

Observe: Turn the paper in different directions. What do you observe about the drawing (like a outsider seeing the drawing for the first time)? What is your first impression? What if you turn it upside down or sideways? Now what do you see that you didn't see before?

Listen: What is the Creator saying? Is it something new or a confirmation? What is He revealing about Himself?

Journal your observations here.

Puzzled Roles

(~30-45 min)

1. Consider the primary roles you embody in life. (e.g. coach, cross-cultural worker, dad). List them out in the space provided.

2. Draw a heart in whatever creative style you desire.

3. Inside the heart, draw various puzzle-piece shapes and sizes (~8-12), each one representing the roles you play out.

4. Fill in the names of the roles, including any that you want to live out that are not yet realized, or are currently "in hiding".

5. Use size to represent the quantity (time/energy) spent in each role, and color as you desire, to set them apart. It's okay to leave some pieces blank, as well.

6. Finish by filling in the the cracks with a color of gold or yellow.

COACHING QUESTION:

When I look at this visual, what does it reflect about my current roles, and how puzzled or clear they are? What part of your unique wiring are you not utilizing right now? What other insights do you gain? Which parts of your roles connect to your calling?

Puzzled Roles

:: INSPIRATION ::

The Japanese art of kintsugi is what inspired this metaphor of a puzzle-piece heart. In this art form, one is taught that objects of pottery—such as a bowl or teapot—when broken, can be repaired with precious metals, such as liquid gold, ultimately creating a stronger bond than the original ceramic. The art teaches that brokenness and the process of repair can actually strengthen the original work, making it more unique and stable in the journey though having gold poured into the cracks. The object actually grows in beauty through the now obvious but brilliant evidence of its brokenness! The cracks in the pottery are looked at as "refined scars". In transition, our identity is challenged to the core. Our hearts are vulnerable and can feel like they are broken and may never heal. Yet, like this art, our times of brokenness can create even greater strength, allowing the refined scars to shine through, illuminating more of the unique masterpiece that is within each one of us.

OPENING OF EYES

That day I saw beneath dark clouds
the passing light over the water
and I heard the voice of the world speak out.
I knew then, as I had before
life is no passing memory of what has been
nor the remaining pages in a great book
waiting to be read.
It is the opening of eyes long closed.
It is the vision of far off things
seen for the silence they hold.
It is the heart after years
of secret conversing
speaking out loud in the clear air.

It is Moses in the desert
fallen to his knees before the lit bush.
It is the man throwing away his shoes
as if to enter heaven
and finding himself astonished,
opened at last,
fallen in love with solid ground.

— David Whyte

Empowering Roles

(~20-30 min)

1. Using your roles listed out from the previous exercise (Puzzled Roles), consider how fruitful you are in each of these roles.

2. Create a grid with a visual metaphor added at the top to represent life-giving fruitfulness. (i.e. fruitful trees vs. dead trees, or smiley faces vs. frowns) Where do you see fruit?

3. List ALL your roles in the left column.

4. For each role, ask the question, "Is this a life-giving role?" Write one short statement for each role, corresponding to its level of empowerment for you currently. (e.g. Cross-cultural worker: struggling, need more language & local friends)

5. Add any roles you don't currently have that you might be interested in exploring more. Add a statement or feeling to reflect this desire.

COACHING QUESTION:

What is highlighted for you about your enjoyment and fruitfulness in your roles? About which roles can you say "I would do this role even if I weren't paid for it?"

Empowering Roles

:: INSPIRATION ::

What would you do for a living, even if you didn't get paid for it?

When we were children, we were frequently asked, "What do you want to be when you grow up?" The assumption was that it would be something enjoyable and life-giving. Yet as we age, for many reasons, we lose sight of the dreams that brought us into the work we have chosen. We forget what we are passionate about. And the shift from, "What do I value and love?" changes to "What will pay the bills?"

What are the measures of fulfillment in your work? For me, the list includes the idea of working in a fulfilling life-giving career where there is more joy than stress; being in a place where my voice is welcome; where I can creatively contribute, using my gifts and strengths, and ultimately get paid for it! There are a number of ways to measure this; but for me the visual of "success" was best represented in the form of a fruit-bearing tree. I want my life to be filled with fruitfulness.

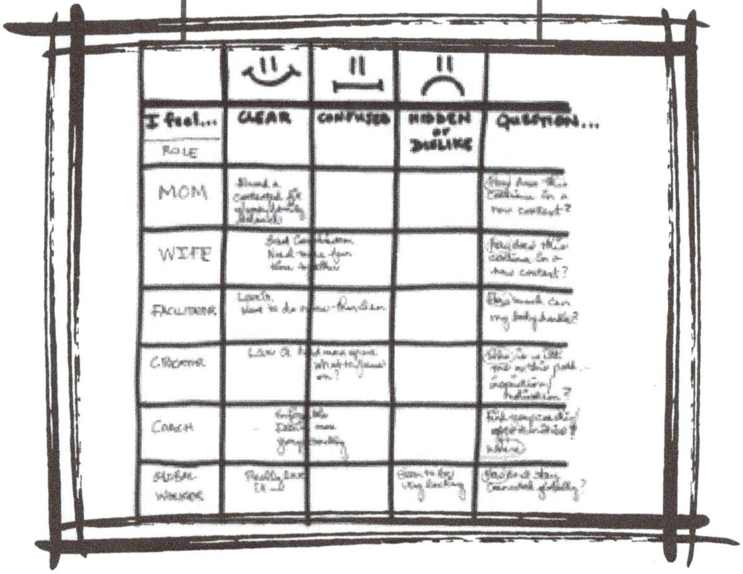
I feel...
ROLE
CLEAR
CONFUSED
HIDDEN or DISLIKE
QUESTION...
MOM
WIFE
FACILITATOR
CREATOR
COACH
GLOBAL WALKER

God sends every person into
the world with a special message to deliver,
with a special song to sing for others,
with a special act of love to bestow.
No one else can speak my message or
sing my song or offer my act of love.
These are entrusted only to me.

— John Powell

100% of the Time

(~20 mins)

1. Consider your average week (168 hours total). Sleep accounts for 56 hours on average. We will round up to 68 to include other rest times. So, 100 hours are available for activity.

2. Create a 100-square grid or represent 100 in a different creative way (see examples on the following pages)

3. Using your current identified roles from the Puzzled Roles exercise, assign each role a color.

4. Consider what percentage of any given week you spend on each role out of 100%. (e.g. Coach: 10% of an average week is spent in this primary role)

5. One example provided, the sun is made up of 100 pixel boxes. You can use this shape if desired to fill in 1 box per 1% of your weekly time use in each role with each assigned color.

COACHING QUESTION:

Does the visual demonstration of color expose any new insights into your energy use, expectations, disconnects, or the areas that seem right, wrong, missing or confused? Reference the Journey Game tool if/as needed.

100% of the Time

:: INSPIRATION ::

Parker Palmer reminds us in *Let Your Life Speak*: "We all arrive on this earth with a gift to share. In our gifted form we have something to offer the world. The form takes a different shape for each person." When I was challenged to think about the accumulated months of an average lifespan, and the average of 60 working years, the time remaining to work with can feel much more pressing! Calculating an allotted (and generous) 4 weeks of annual vacation time, the total number of working months = 660; or 2,880 weeks! I needed to break down the numbers one step further to consider how I am using my time on a weekly basis—I have approximately 100 hours of "awake" time per week!. When these weeks, months and years of my life were represented visually, it hit me quite significantly. How am I being a wise steward of my time? How am I living out the precious hours that I have been given? I've occasionally used the metaphor of a clock (60 minutes = 1 working year for every minute). But for now the cubic representation of a "life landscape" resonated with me. Feel free to find your own creative way to break things down...

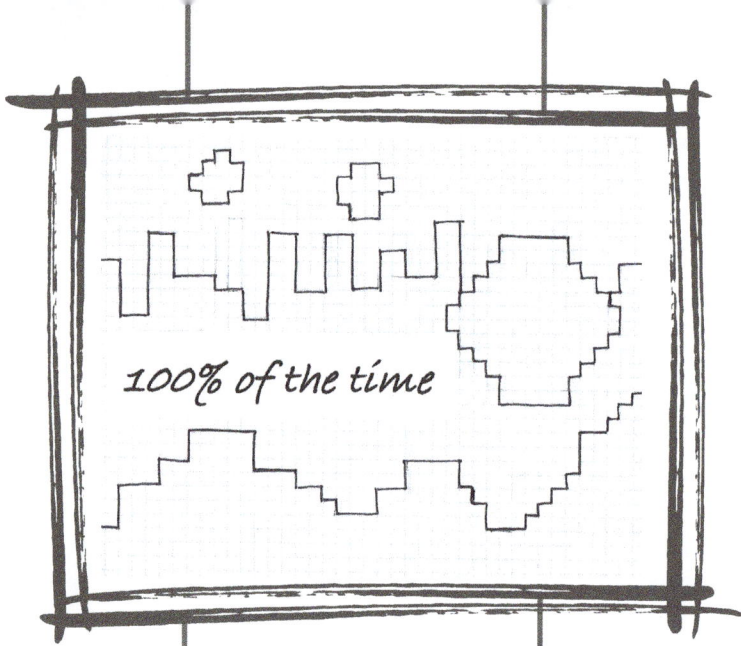

100% of the time

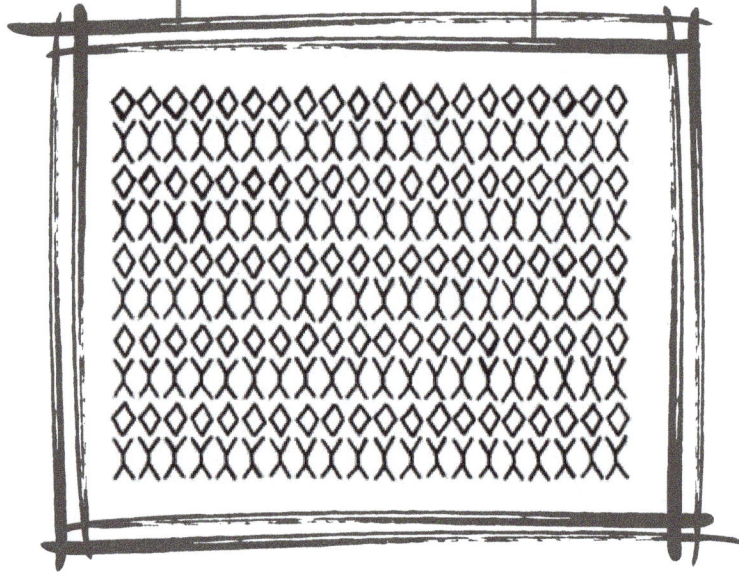

Limitations

Real knowing of ourselves can only occur after we are convinced that we are deeply loved precisely as we are.

— David Benner

(~20 min)

Surrender

Raise your arms slightly out at shoulder length with palms facing upward. Stay in this position, or eventually reach up toward the sky. Feel free to vary between these two postures as you feel led. Alternatively, you can kneel and take child's pose (yoga style), or lay prostrate. Reflect on what you're holding onto and need to release, or surrender to God.

Why

A posture of surrender reminds us that we are not in charge; the Creator is. He wants us to join Him in the plans He has for our life.

Reflect

How does this posture feel to you?

POSTURE OF
Surrender

Body Scan & Blessing

GUIDELINES:

Body Scan & Blessing

(~20 min)

While walking or sitting, do a body scan. A scan is like an x-ray looking for areas of pain. Starting from a meditative posture, and breathing, begin by choosing one end of your body to start with. Bring awareness to the feelings of pain or discomfort in your body. Stop in the places where there is pain and bless these areas. Call forth life and strength into them. Have a conversation with that part of your body as to where the pain might be coming from.

Move on with the scan after each short conversation.

What is the weight that your body is carrying?

Where are the sources in life producing pain for you?

Where do you feel good and strong?

Reflect. How is it for you to be intentionally attending to your body in this way?

Praying in Color

Praying in Color

(~20 min)

Choose a pencil or colored pencils of your liking.

Write the word "calling" or "work" in the middle of the paper that follows.

Begin creating a shape of your choosing around it. Without analyzing or judging, invite other words and shapes to join the page.

Let it grow like a free-flowing or abstract doodle. Trace, draw and let your pencil lead the way.

Meanwhile, let yourself feel the drawing and the words. Do they feel heavy, light, joyful, anxiety producing?

In prayer, ask, What is troubling me or bringing me joy about this?

Let the shapes and color represent those feelings as you continue drawing. At the same time converse with God around these words, as your counselor or coach.

Ask: What is troubling me, or joy-giving, about this?

How do you want me to see this?

How do you want to join me in this?

How do you want me to continue to engage with it?

Journal any thoughts or feelings that stand out to you.

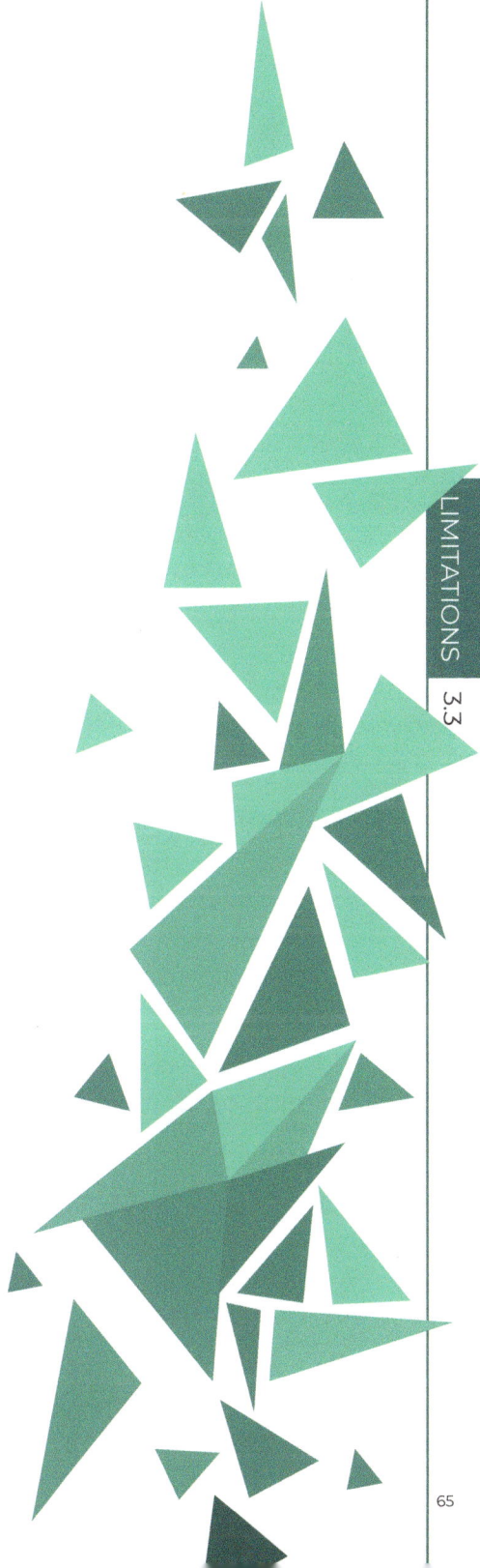

Self-Care Wheel part I

(~20 min)

Similar to the body scan, do an overview of life scan. Ask: How am I doing in the following categories?

· **Physical needs**—Do I have what I need to healthily eat, sleep, clothe and care for myself—the basics of life? Am I settled in where I live? Are my kids cared for? Are we safe?

· **Emotional social support**—Are there people who I can, and DO, share my thoughts and feelings with? Do I have empathic listeners in my life?

· **Financial**—Are my basic needs adequately covered financially? Do I have a clear and realistic budget, and am I following it? Am I able to invest for the future?

· **Spiritual vitality**—Am I actively developing my spiritual life? Do I feel close or far away from my Creator at this season? Am I involved in life-giving community that help to mature my faith walk?

· **Vocational fulfillment**—How does my life and work have meaning? Do I receive feedback on my work? Am I developing?

· **Emotional play**—Am I able to regularly engage in life-giving hobbies, sport or play?

1. Do an overview of life scan.
2. Evaluate each of the 6 categories using this scale: Disempowering, Liability, Solid and Empowering.
3. Create a horizontal line. From left to right add the words disempowering, liability, solid and empowering. Plot where you land in each category using a word or symbol.

Disempowering = Detracts from focus & goals; needs immediate attention

Liability = Sufficient to get by. At risk, especially in times of stress

Solid = Satisfied. Does not currently carry any risk of liability

Empowering = There is enough to share with others. Utilize empowering categories to elevate disempowering categories

4. See example on the next page

Self-Care Wheel
PART I

:: INSPIRATION ::

Maslow's Hierarchy of Needs & Social Base Theory

Have you ever traveled for 24+ hours, to finally arrive at your destination in complete exhaustion, without a care for food or even a toothbrush! A soft bed is the only thing you want. This is a regular example of a "need pyramid" temporarily out of sync. Psychologist Abraham Maslow is known for his theory of the Hierarchy of Innate Human Needs. In this he illustrated that every human operates on a graduated pyramid of needs. "At the base are our physiological needs, such as food, water, and shelter. Only if these needs are met are we prompted to meet our need for safety, then to meet the uniquely human needs to give and receive love and ultimately reach self-actualization in our work."

In clarifying one's skills, talents, and strengths, a person is often motivated to use their unique wiring for the good of others. This awareness gives permission in times of insecurity, stress, or loss—to come back to an equilibrium—the core of who one is uniquely. Having self-awareness about one's unique strengths offers guidance in times of transition, aiding decision-making, and better identifying new goals and ultimately more satisfaction.

J. Robert Clinton, in his book Leadership Emergence Theory, modified Maslow's Hierarchy of Needs in what he terms the Social Base Analysis. Typically used as a self-assessment tool, Clinton assigned four categories to measure how well one is adapting and thriving in his or her environment as a leader. For a more holistic purpose, we have since expanded his categories to six, and named it the "Self-Care Wheel"—Physical, Emotional Support (Social), Financial, Spiritual, Vocational, and Emotional (Play). Healthy people know what they need... and they ask for it.

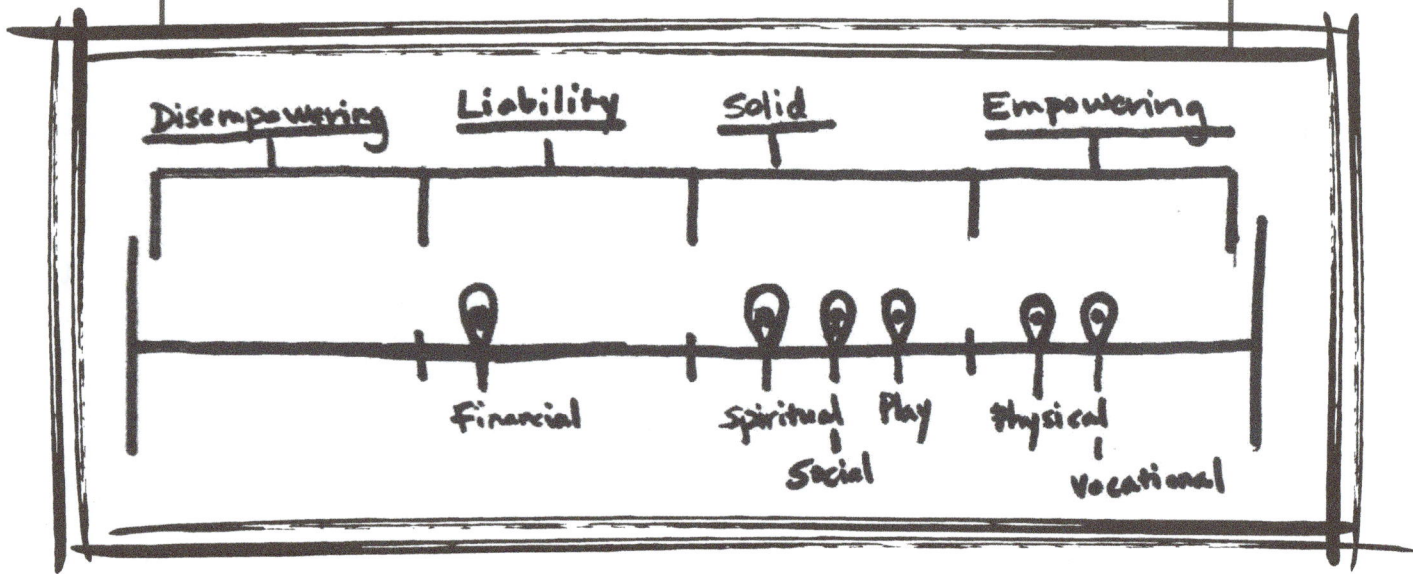

Self-care Wheel part II

(~30 min)

1. Thinking about the felt-difference between life empowered versus life disempowered, utilize a wheel with 6 spokes to represent each of the 6 categories for the self-care wheel: Emotional play, emotional support, spiritual vitality, vocational fulfillment, financial needs met & physical health.

2. Consider your current level of satisfaction with each of the six categories of SUPPORT listed. The center of the wheel represents the lowest level of satisfaction, or "0" on the scale. The outer edge is the highest level of satisfaction.

3. Fill in each section with a color of your choice to represent your current level of satisfaction with the health and presence of that category in your life.

4. Assign one or two words of explanation next to the rating.

5. List one sentence from the coaching questions below next to each of the six sections.

COACHING QUESTION:

What do I need to keep doing? What do I need to stop doing? What do I need to do differently? What do I need to start doing?

Self-Care Wheel
PART II

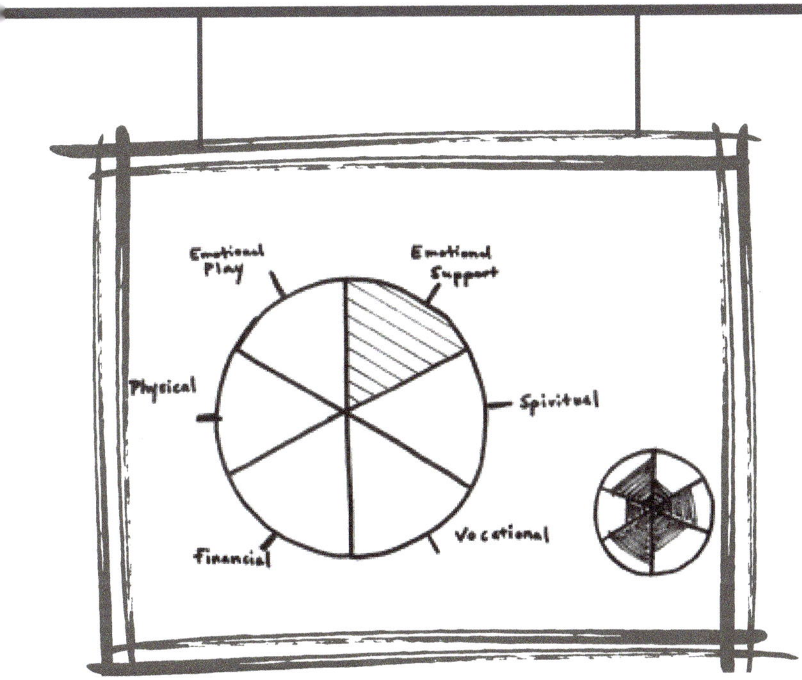

Emotional Play
Emotional Support
Physical
Spiritual
Financial
Vocational

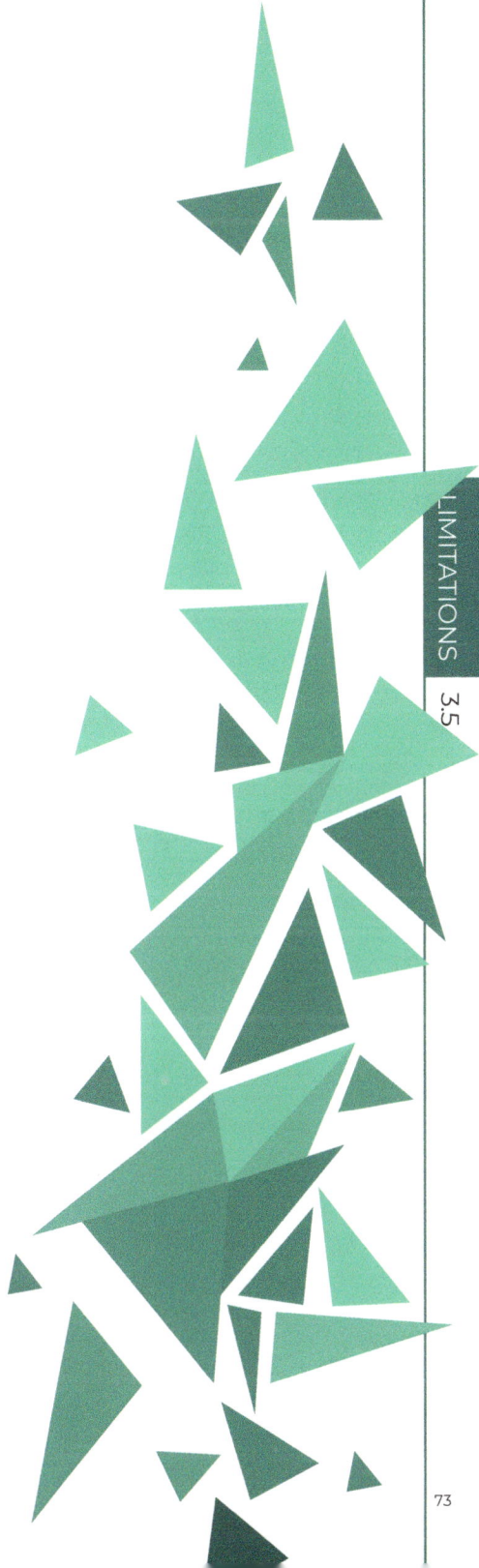

Transition Timeline part I

(~1 hour)

1. Consider the entire course of your life from birth to now.
2. Brainstorm a minimum of 10 turning points in your life. A turning point is defined as one or more significant events that changed the course of your future or the direction of your path. (i.e. getting married, losing a job, moving to a foreign country).
3. As you list these turning points, assign each major event as either a high or low (you may do this with color).
4. Now give each turning point a one or two word description.

COACHING QUESTION:

What patterns do you notice? How does this inform your current transition? What is God trying to teach you about your future through your past?

Transition Timeline
PART I

:: INSPIRATION ::

The seeds of growth for your future can be traced back to significant shaping experiences over the course of your past. Nothing is a mistake in your life. With this in mind, it is important to take time to reflect on how God has worked in, and through, your past. One of the effective ways to capture and view a "lifetime perspective" is to generate a list of key turning points, and to represent them strategically in a unique timeline matrix. This process helps you to glean particular angles of insight regarding God's fingerprints in your journey. The desire here is to reveal key patterns and insights emerging from the tumult of transition seasons. Where the self-care wheel provides a glimpse into the NOW, the transition timeline provides an aerial view and longitudinal perspective into health and balance over several seasons.

In doing this exercise during a major turning point in my life, I gained great advantage through the realization that the same areas of "liability" existed in every transition I had experienced. Was this area of lacking unique to me? Or was there an invitation from God that I was repeatedly missing, but now could receive clearly with better altitude?

The place God calls you is the place where your deep gladness and the world's deep hunger meet.

— Frederick Buechner

Transition Timeline part II

(~30 min)

1. On the following open pages, place a horizontal line in the middle of the paper. This line has a neutral value. Above the line will represent events that you would consider emotionally positive experiences and below it difficult or emotionally low experiences.

2. Looking at your previously-made list of turning points, plot each one with the assigned 1 or 2 words on the timeline. (Try to capture the cumulative emotional experience as best as you remember it. Recognizing many events have a range of both highs and lows).

3. After plotting them all, using colored pencils, visually connect the lines. What if anything do you notice?

Bonus: For deeper reflection, utilize the self-care wheel exercise and assess each major turning point. Create a small wheel at every one noticing which category is most disempowering and which is most empowering.

COACHING QUESTION:

What patterns do you see emerging over the course of your lifetime? How does this information inform your current transition?

Transition Timeline
PART II

Places in the World

(~20 min)

1. As a continuation of your unique timeline, in the space provided, list the places you have called "home" over the course of your lifetime.
2. Create a map of the world.
3. Draw a line out from the map as close as possible to the countries and cities of the different places you have called home. Write the name of each place. (Note: If you moved several times within a city, you can choose how many points you wish to plot.)
4. Assign a number starting with 1 where you were born, chronologically ordering the different plots. Connect the dots starting with number 1.

COACHING QUESTION:

What does this exercise further say to you about your timeline? Are there parts of you that still feel "left" in locations around the globe? How does this exercise inform your dreams/longings for the future?

Places in the World

:: INSPIRATION ::

The visual representation of the globe provides an opportunity to gain new self-awareness as you consider your presence on this Earth. The moves you've made (or not), the languages learned (or not), the places of connection with your heart.

I love what Tim Keller says about being messengers in this world: "There are particular things for you to do and particular people that you are to help. You have been shaped to be the instrument of healing. Your experiences, your joy, your sorrows, your race, your age, your gender, your gift mix — all shaped you for some hands that only you can hold, some needs only you can meet, some demons only you can drive out, certain people God has prepared for you to be the healing agent in their lives."

If you're a global worker, you are likely reminded that this earth is not your ultimate home. What strikes you when you look at your "homes" represented in a visual and global form? Are there parts of you that are already trying to move to a different or new place?

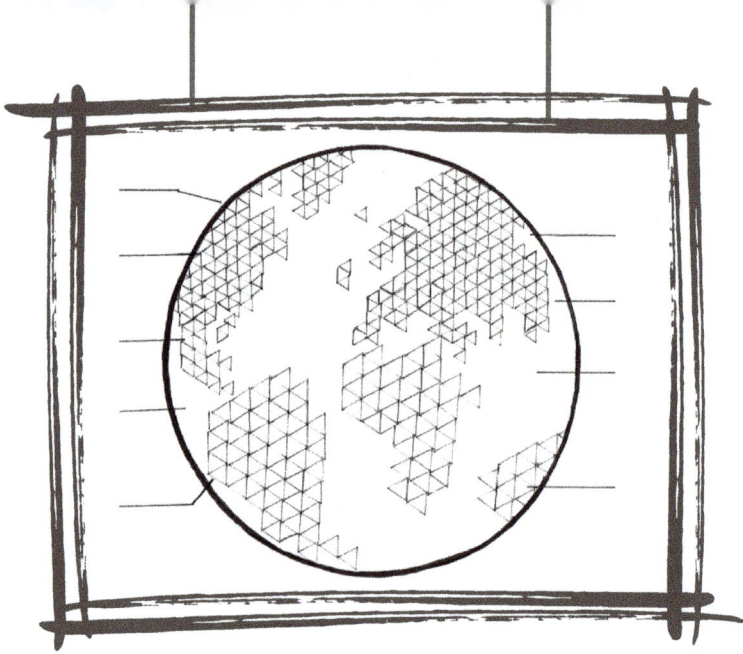

Reconciliation

Body Prayer

Jesus was not

resurrected to what he was,

But was re-created into

something new,

the risen glorified Christ

Is there a reconciliation

that needs to be completed

Before I am made like my Lord?

I will seek reconciliation;

I will go where I need to go to find it;

I ASK THAT IT BE EXPOSED TO ME

"May the Lord be pleased with my desire for wholeness"

In relationship, in grace, in the way of Jesus.

God grant me the wisdom, the courage to

know how to best reconcile with each person,

Whether the time is right,

and how to speak the truth in love.

Peace is ahead of my steps; it will be waiting for me.

— Pagitt & Prill

POSTURE OF
Reconciliation

:: POSTURE ::

(~20 min)

Reconciliation

Position: Stand with your arms and legs relaxed.

Why?

It's God's hope and desire that all of creation be reconciled. With God and with one another. This kind of reconciliation takes hard work and at times requires death and rebirth. Pain often accompanies this bringing together in ways that can seem overwhelming. At times reconciliation means moving towards someone or something. Other times it means stillness with dependence on God's reconciling work on the cross.

Reflect

Do you feel like you are being invited to move or stand still as it relates to reconciliation?

Shaping of the Cross

(~20 min)

This is a simple whole body exercise where you will shape an invisible cross using your body while silently talking to God.

Start by playing some music. (I suggest *Meet Joe Black* put on repeat 3 or 4 times.)

Stand up and **Imagine**.

When you reach the top, **follow** the shape of the cross back down to where you started.

Trace the shape of a cross that comes naturally to you. Stop at any point and repeat as many times as you like.

Reflect, how was it to engage your body in this way?

Journal or draw any reflections you want to capture in the space provided.

Shaping of the Cross

Blind Visual

(~20 min)

Center Yourself: Relax and take a few deep, slow breaths.

Invite the Creator: To fill you with peace and guide you as you think about your current transition.

Set a timer for 15 minutes.

Start by drawing with your eyes closed. Use only lines and shapes, no symbols or intentional pictures. You can lift your pencil, but it may be easier not to.

Remember: This is an abstract drawing. When you are done, look at it from different angles. Turn the paper upside down and consider the meaning from different directions.

Observe: How did it feel doing this "blind"?

Journal in the space provided.

Blind Visual

Cross of Recociliation

(~30-45 min)

1. Draw a cross with as much or as little detail as you'd like.
2. Consider someone with whom you are currently struggling. (i.e. yourself, God, another person).
3. As you draw, let the color express heaviness, negativity, ways you are hurt or have been wronged.
4. As you think of words, list them on one side of the cross. These might include thoughts or feelings, ways you've been hurt or wronged, things you dislike about the person. Let negative and angry thoughts be welcome but not take over.
5. Now consider your part in the relationship. Ways that you have done wrong or hurt another. This may require time and a posture of humility with others or the Lord. List your contribution on the other side.
6. When the ability to authentically release or forgive comes from God, cross off the offense on either side listed.
7. Take the necessary time required for this process. It may be something you come back to over the course of weeks or create more than once.
8. As you reflect, consider what comes up for you in reconciliation that is unique to this transition?

COACHING QUESTION:

What is God inviting you to take steps towards reconciliation in, in this particular season?

Cross of Reconciliation

:: **INSPIRATION** ::

While discussing an area of deep hurt with a wise mentor, Bill Randall, the suggestion arose to take the hurt and the pain to the cross. Likely not once. But repeatedly and whenever needed. The proposition was to create my own cross and to write how I had done wrong on one side and how I had felt wronged by the other person on the other side. Integral to the process was the assumption that I had a part in it (confession) and likewise that there was another offender as well (forgiveness); but that the entirety was to be left at the cross where it was already "finished" regardless of if the other ever spoke a single utterance of remorse.

Drawing out the cross allowed me to process the pain, and pray with great lament. "These are all the ways I was wronged" And yet simultaneously with an abundance of grace, I repeatedly was brought back to Psalm 139. Prompted to present my part in it. The ability to release came from the strength of the Lord. The ability to keep releasing remains a daily invitation to my gracious redeemer's side.

Cross of Reconciliation Example

God, I invite your searching gaze into my heart.
Examine me through and through;
find out everything that may be hidden within me.
Put me to the test and sift through all my anxious cares. See if
there is any path of pain I'm walking on,   *and*
lead me back to your glorious,
everlasting ways – the path that brings me back to you.

– Psalm 139 TPT

Remembering

(~30 min)

The purpose of these pages is to reflect on the words, dreams, prophecies, pictures, or songs that have been a part of your journey. They may have come directly to you, from scripture or from others.

Remembering is a discipline that leads us directly back to gratitude. The simple act of remembering takes us out of our limited view to that of a much greater perspective.

Draw or write in the images provided.

Note: Come back to this as you take part in the rest of this process, naming the many ways that you've received clarity in direction

COACHING QUESTION:

How has God spoken to you in the past? What is He saying in this particular season of transition?

Remembering

Remembering is what gives me
vision for the future
— Alabaster Co.

Map Your Network part I

(~30 min)

1. Consider who are the people that are supporting you in this transition? Who are the people who celebrate your gifts with you?
2. Consider this network of people that you uniquely have in your life helping you, for example with your self-care wheel.
3. Draw a map like a neighborhood. This is your community regardless of real life proximity. Your "neighbors" are these caring people.
4. Use objects (trees, windows, etc), color, shapes, and shading to represent each person or category.
5. As an exercise in gratitude, give thanks for this support system

COACHING QUESTION:

What social support network do you notice is in abundance or lacking? Who do you know who can currently aide you in your next steps going forward?

Map Your Network
PART I

:: INSPIRATION ::

Mr Roger's Neighborhood was an influential show when I was little. Whether because he was so kind or the themes were so simple, I watched it every day.

In my most recent transition, I was given the gift of an incredible support network; like a neighborhood full of kind and caring neighbors. I felt that they were often the structure supporting me like the foundation of a house. Without so many amazing, and caring people I don't know how I would have made it through.

Consider the role of your community supporting you in this transition. Who are the people that are cheering you on? Who are the people who celebrate your gifts and strengths alongside of you?

Map Your Network part II

(Time Varies)

A valuable part of discernment and decision-making is the voice that your community plays in your life. Utilizing the feedback questions in the appendix, ask 3-5 trusted and non-biased individuals to answer these questions on your behalf.

On the following pages provided, divide your paper in half. On one half list the advice or input that you feel is consistent with yourself, God and others. On the other half put any messages that are conflicting or need further exploration. This space exists as a space to both record & sort their feedback and any important themes that the individuals may speak into your life.

COACHING QUESTION:

What input have your received from trusted sources about your transition that you want to make note of? What patterns did you notice? What, if any conflicting messages do you need to follow up on?

Map Your Network
PART II

Dreams

*Vocation does not come from a voice
"out there" calling me to become something
I am not. It comes from a voice
"in here" calling me to be the
person I was born to be,
to fulfill the original self-hood
given me at birth by God.*

— Parker Palmer

DREAMS

:: POSTURE ::

(~20 min)

Guidance

Position
Sitting cross-legged; engage your head and neck by bowing forward or raising to heaven.

Why?
Guidance is a universal and never-ending need. Everyone looking for clarity, guidance and direction is really looking for God. To seek guidance from God is really to seek God. We are not asking for input, we are asking for intimacy.

Reflect
How does this posture resonate with you in this season?

Communal Body Blessing

(~30 min)

(This exercise is done in silence)

Similar to the Body Scan/Blessing exercise, you will continue the same exercise by doing this with one other person or a group.

Sitting facing each other or in a circle, choose one person to start. With his/her eyes closed the first person begins by scanning his/her body to consider where there is pain. Starting from the feet up. He/she will place their hands on their own body where there is pain. Others in the trusted circle will place their hands on their own body mirroring the pain of the person in the middle and praying on their behalf. Stay for several seconds in each place where there is pain. As soon as the first person has gone all the way through his/her body. They will communicate without words to the next person to take a turn (or pass).

How is this different doing something like this with another person or persons?

After both people, or the group has finished, share out loud any unique words, sensations or pictures that you received for each other.

Communal Body Blessing

Labyrinth

(~20 min)

1. Find a labyrinth. Whether a life-size version or a simple one you can trace with your finger.
2. Form a question you are grappling with at this point or use "What am I afraid of?
3. As you begin to enter the labyrinth ask for His presence with you in this experience letting go of other distractions.
4. Stay open to whatever feelings, sensations, ideas come.
5. Pause at any time to breathe, focus or just to relax.
6. At the center of the labyrinth, sense your connection to your own center and to the centering presence of God. Receive at the center whatever wisdom or guidance you're asking for. Acknowledge the Creator as heavenly counselor
7. Breathe, relax, pray or sing, repeat!
8. When you're ready, begin to exit continuing to discuss your question in prayer; Consciously returning & bringing the wisdom into your life.
9. Reflect on how this process is for you.

COACHING QUESTION:

What do I need to release, that I received from this centering exercise, as I step back into my life?

Labyrinth

Labyrinth Prayer

God almighty,
holy and loving one,
eternal, ever-present one,
walk with us.

Earth maker, life giver,
pain bearer,
lover of our souls,
walk with us.

Through all the twists
and turns of life,
when clouds obscure the way,
walk with us.

When what once seemed close
now looks so far away,
walk with us.
Light bringer, faith builder,
justice bringer,
walk with us,

until we trust in you,
and walk the path
that leads to the center of
your love
walk with us.

— Christine Sine

Being original is not about generating something out of nothing. It is taking ideas from one place and applying them in a new way.

— Dr. D. Eagleman

Limiting Beliefs

Limiting Beliefs

(~30 min)

As you engage with the artistic side of you, many voices from the past may bubble up. Note them and come back to them later. Don't give them undue attention that they might demand; but also don't wholly ignore them.

This exercise is a created "visual parking lot" for your distractions, lies, and negative-self beliefs.

1. As lies come up, write a word or two to represent them on the "I AM NOT" side of the paper.
2. As you come back to them for each "I AM NOT" lie or negative belief create an opposing "I AM" statement of affirmation.
3. For each lie or negative belief begin blacking them out with a dark colored pencil. For each truth add color of light. You will end up with a picture of contrast light and darkness.
4. Ask someone you trust to tell you how they see your gifts at work in this world.
5. Ask God to help you to internalize the truth of how He sees you and what you bring to the world.

I AM...

I AM NOT...

Head in the Clouds

(~30 min)

1. Think through your roles (puzzled heart & enjoyable roles), use each hat you'd like to be wearing 5 years from now and brainstorm possibilities of what it could look like.
2. Consider your longings, dreams, hopes and desires for your future contribution and legacy. What would you like to contribute as a father, a worker using your calling, a son, or a friend?
3. Draw your head in the clouds picturing the many possibilities without limitations.

Coaching question:

What decision, place, opportunity will most help me become the person I long to become? Where might I enjoy God most?

Head in the Clouds

:: INSPIRATION ::

When God created Adam, He invited him to imagine without limits the possibilities of all the names of the animals. He didn't limit him to a core set of rules. Instead the Creator of the universe invited man to the task of imagining without limits the name of each living creature! (Genesis 2).

Likewise, God still invites us to be part of the creative process. He wants us to imagine without limit the possibilities of our future. In the Art of Life Planning, an inspiration for this work, my mentor Buck Rogers inquires, 'Without limitations, what possibilities can you imagine in each of your different roles? And where are your longings?"

Difficult for some is the consideration of uninhibited potential. For others the space to consider the future allows for an imaginative play time. When adding color and drawing creatively the imagination is unleashed to explore further. I'm inspired to explore – whether to explore the possibilities or to explore the blocks. A place to consider the possibilities without refrain.

Decision-making

(~45 min)

1. Make a table to represent your top 4-5 choices for your futures (a 5x5 table for example)

2. Assign a number and identify with an abbreviation the titles of your top choices in the top row and far left column. The list will be the same on the left side as the top.

3. Put X's on the numbers that coincide as you won't be comparing 1 vs. 1 or 2 vs. 2

4. Now go through each row. When you compare number 1 to number 2, ask "which option more accurately aligns with my/our future desires? My personality & strengths? And our needs (self-care wheel?) Note: You've already done the hard work... Don't over-analyze. Go with your gut at this point.

5. Write the number chosen between the two options in the box. You will be comparing the same things twice, for example 2 vs. 4 and 4 vs. 2 it's okay to change your mind or have a split.

6. After you've gone through the whole table, count up how many of each number you have:

   1 - __, 2 - __, 3-__, 4-__, 5-__, 6-__

7. You should have a number with more answers than all the rest

8. Consider how this option sounds; sit with it; ask others; pray about it.

COACHING QUESTION:

What obvious blocks come into place? What important questions still need answering?
What information do you still need to gather?

Decision-making

:: INSPIRATION ::

Coming down from the clouds of possibilities requires a certain abrupt-feeling of grounding, and simultaneously an invitation to keep looking up into the clouds. When I see a skyscraper I'm amazed and in awe of the design and what it took to actualize such a grand structure; a great focus on the end goal – both a looking up and down at the same time.

Utilizing a decision-making grid can help one to begin to make concrete the seemingly unlimited possibilities. Synthesizing the possibilities, came in part from the inspiration in Halftime by Bob Buford. Here were my choices:

1. Keep doing what I already do well but change the environment
2. Change the work, but stay in the same environment
3. Turn an avocation into a new career
4. Parallel career
5. Get more training
6. Keep on doing the same thing

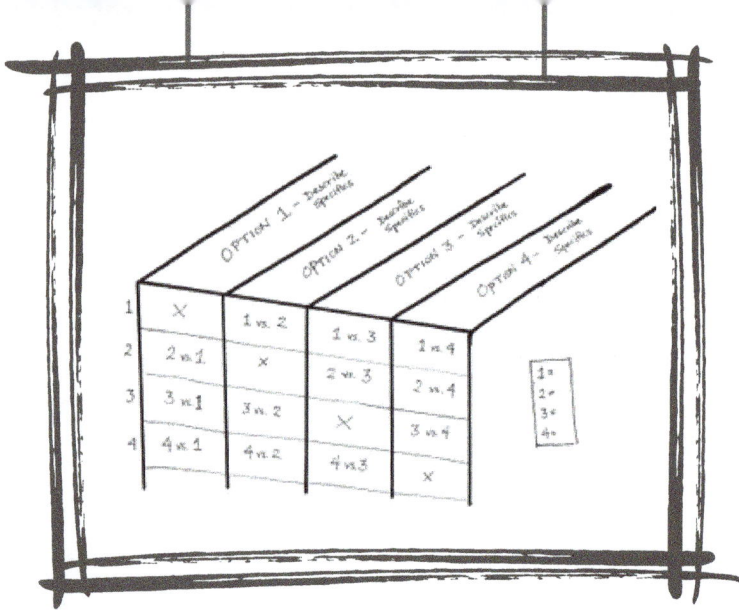

	OPTION 1 – Describe Specifics	OPTION 2 – Describe Specifics	OPTION 3 – Describe Specifics	OPTION 4 – Describe Specifics
1	X	1 vs. 2	1 vs. 3	1 vs. 4
2	2 vs. 1	X	2 vs. 3	2 vs. 4
3	3 vs. 1	3 vs. 2	X	3 vs. 4
4	4 vs. 1	4 vs. 2	4 vs. 3	X

1°
2°
3°
4°

New Moves

Life is a creative,
intimate and unpredictable
conversation if it is nothing else,
spoken or unspoken, & our life & work
are both the result of the
particular way we hold
the passionate conversation.

– David Whyte

Self-Selected POSTURE

:: POSTURE ::

(~30 min)

Self-selected

Position
Which posture have you felt most drawn to? Choose any of the postures done thus far or a different one that has most resonated with you to continue to use as you move into your next steps

Why?
Ask God to meet you in this position of prayer

Reflect
How does this posture feel to you?

Life is no brief candle to me.
It is a sort of splendid torch
which I've got ahold of for the moment,
and I want to make it burn
as brightly as possible before
handing it on to
future generations.

— George Bernard Shaw

Mirroring

Mirroring

(~30 min)

Choose the prayer posture that most resonates with how you want to continue meeting with God in this season.

In a safe small group, one at a time, **share** WITHOUT words your chosen posture.

Every other person will **mirror** and hold the posture for at least 30 seconds.

Similar to how posturing ourselves physically before God allows us to more deeply intercede, mirroring other's postures allows us to carry the weight of their burdens.

Reflect out loud after the exercise how the experience was different from simply sharing with words.

Example:

Statements selected
1. "we need each other for balance"
2. "we are not a man"
3. "we all embody beauty"
4. "we are all learning to find a
   place & a voice"
5. "we are complex"
6. "we are on a long journey of
   trust"

Poem
[1] We need each other for balance
[2] We are not a man
[3] We all embody beauty
[4] We are all learning to find a
     place & a voice

[2] We are not a man
[5] We are complex
[4] We are all learning to find a
     place & a voice
[6] We are on a long journey of
     trust

[5] We are complex
[3] We all embody beauty
[6] We are on a long journey of
     trust
[1] We need each other for balance

Poetry of Lament

Poetry of Lament

(~30 min)

1. Begin by free-writing. Write out in short paragraph form your thoughts & feelings relating to your body, life, or current circumstances.
2. Underline 6 statements that stand out to you as significant. Assign each statement a number 1 – 6.
3. Arrange them in this format:

   Stanza 1: #1,2,3,4
   Stanza 2: #2,5,4,6
   Stanza 3: #5,3,6,1

(from The Artist's Rule)

A thief has only
one thing in mind—
be wants to steal,
slaughter and destroy.
But I have come to give
you everything in abundance,
more than you expect—
life in its fullness
until you overflow!

— John 10:10 TPT

Working Backwards

(~30 min)

What courage is required of you TODAY?

1. Consider for a moment all of the processing you've done up until now! – The Journey Game, Unique Wiring, Puzzled Roles, Enjoyable Roles, Self-care wheel, Transition timeline, places in the world, Cross of Reconciliation, head in the clouds

2. Draw a mountain, steps or something that symbolizes a difficult task requiring increments or steps.

3. Answer first, "what would you like your life to look like 5 years from now? Write 2-3 statements at the top.

4. What would need to be in place 3 years from now in order for you obtain your 5-year vision? Write it at the next level.

5. What would you need to do 1 year from now to be on track for 3 years and 5 years?

6. What do you need to do 3 months from now to be on track for 1 year, 3 years, and 5 years?

COACHING QUESTION:

What information do you need to gather to make further decisions? What action steps can you take THIS WEEK or THIS MONTH in order to continue looking ahead to your ideal self in 5 years?

Working Backwards

As an avid hiker, the metaphor of a mountain top encompasses the challenge of the process and the elation of the summit. Not many achieve these great under-takings. Those that do, have typically undergone intentional training & proper preparation. They know that the tools & resources they implement will allow for the ease of the execution and a greater opportunity for success.

Attempting to capture all that was gained in this process, the aim of this tool is to break down what take-aways are most important for you. The inspiration stems from my coaching background and creating concrete next steps rather than leaving them to fate! When the process is holistic coming back from a bird's-eye view requires landing with intentionality.

Trust is hard since you
have nothing to fall back on.
The new country is where
you are called to go,
and the only way to go there
is naked and vulnerable.
Maybe you don't recognize
the way because
you are going somewhere
you have not been.
Maybe you are coming home.

— Henri J. M. Nouwen

Continuing

During the most painful times of transition—during moments of intense darkness—all I could naturally do was process, analyze and over-process my situation. In actuality I became obsessed with thoughts of what was said or not said, done or not done. I knew the answer for how to approach my future was somewhere in me if only I could figure it out. If only I could think my way into it—like my strategic-minded analytic self normally could! However, in that season my brain would not let me. My brain and body left me short-sighted and frustrated in these circumstances. This over-analysis only created greater frustration and paralysis, my normal modes of operating fell short...

What to do with your blocks?

Being stuck is a normal part of every creative process. Don't panic. Several exercises we have done were meant to aide in unlocking creativity. Anything that accesses your right brain more such as games, exercise, or habits of daily life like walking, driving, or washing dishes, all allow for greater integration and ability to conceptualize a way forward differently. Learn which simple tasks move you from the stuck cycle into new insight and inspiration. Try on different exercises at different times. And come back to your new toolbox in future transitions.

We all need some extra support at times. Utilize TheWayBetween.org/blog or implement a personalized transition coaching for continued growth.

Your Story

Where did you find yourself wanting to stay throughout this process? Which stuck tools do you want to keep incorporating during your transition? How will you keep that a regular practice?"

Appendices

Sources

- The Art of Life Planning — [Buck Rogers]
- All That is Made: A Guide to Faith and the Creative Life — [Alabaster Co.]
- The Artist's Rule: Nurturing Your Creative Soul with Monastic Wisdom — [Christine Valters Palmer]
- The Artist's Way: A Spiritual Path to Higher Creativity — [Julia Cameron]
- The Body Keeps the Score: Brain, Mind and Body in the Healing of Trauma — [Bessel VanDerKolk]
- Body Prayer: The Posture of Intimacy with God — [Doug Pagitt & Kathryn Prill]
- Courage and Calling: Embracing Your God-Given Potential — [Gordon Smith]
- The Discover Your True North Fieldbook — [Craig, George & Snook]
- The Doodle Revolution: Unlock the Power to Think Differently — [Sunni Brown]
- Draw Near Visual Prayer — [Sandee Hunt]
- Draw Your Big Idea — [Nora Herting & Heather Willems]
- Drawing with Your Artist's Brain — [Carl Purcell]
- The Gift of Being Yourself: The Sacred Call to Self-Discovery — [David Benner]
- The Land Between: Finding God in Difficult Transitions — [Jeff Manion]
- Let Your Life Speak: Listening for the Voice of Vocation — [Parker J. Palmer]
- Living a Life that Counts — [Tom Patterson]
- The Making of a Leader: Recognizing the Lessons & Stages of Leadership Development — [J. Robert Clinton]
- Necessary Endings — [Henry Cloud]
- Praying in Color: Drawing a New Path to God — [Sybil MacBeth]
- The Rest of God: Restoring Your Soul by Restoring Sabbath — [Mark Buchanan]
- The Road Back to You: An Enneagram Journey to Self-Discovery — [Ian Morgan Cron & Suzanne Stabile]
- Stuck!: Navigating the Transitions of Life & Leadership — [Terry Walling]
- Understanding Yourself and Others Series: The 16 Personality Types — [Berens & Nardi]
- The Way of Transition: Embracing Life's Difficult Moments — [William Bridges]

Why art and movement?

Why an expressive arts workbook for transition?

Major life transition often includes a myriad of decisions but comes at a time when information density is high and processing capacity typically low. The engagement of the whole brain while strategically planning aides in clarity and deeper awareness. Inviting the creative and logic brains to work together helps get past the hurdles where we typically get "stuck" during transition. Utilizing art and movement allows us to fully engage ourselves through an alternative access door.

Art connects us to our childlike wonder and awe of the way the world around us works. I believe we are ALL created creative. Some of us just access the artistic side of our brain more regularly. Drawing is the most universal and basic of all art forms. It invites us to express thoughts and feelings without the barriers of written language, opening new doors to the imagination. Ultimately, drawing stimulates the whole brain, allowing for deeper integration of processing and decision-making.

Why include body movement?

In a deeply visceral way, our body is our unique guide & teacher along the journey. We must learn to "study it", "read it" and "listen" to what it is teaching us. The body instinctively knows how to move, stop for rest, and breathe deeply. Sometimes we have to re-train it to do these core functions—especially after a trauma, through periods of intense grief or re-occurring seasons of stress. In times of deep pain, our body owns and carries heavy emotions, causing us to ask questions unique to suffering, and moves us to seek a higher power outside of the capacity of our own strength and will. Our ears are more greatly attuned when we experience the visceral reaction of pain rather than simply reading about it or learning it from others. Natural questions asked by those in physical and chronic suffering are significantly different from that of an individual not in a season of trial

Regardless of the method, engaging both art and movement together, provide an opportunity for integration of our whole brain—our whole self.

As you pick up this book, I encourage you to embrace and ENJOY the beautiful journey ahead of you, as you engage your creative side, meet with the Creator, and in turn, find new platforms for your voice and clarity in this season of transition!

What to do with blocks?

There are several exercises in this section meant to aide in unlocking creativity. We use them in The Art of Transition workshop as warm-up exercises to ultimately allow for greater focus and depth. Any regular and repetitive action helps to prime the well—needlework, walking, driving, washing dishes. Learn which "simple" tasks work best for you and use them! It may be helpful to effectively invite and move yourself into the drawing process and the "getting unstuck" times - ultimately opening the windows to new insight and inspiration.

As you engage with the artistic side of you, many voices from the past may bubble up. Note any limiting beliefs in the sub-section titled limiting beliefs under the dreams section. We will come back to them later. Don't give them undue attention that they might demand; but also don't wholly ignore them. Come back to these exercises as often as you need. We all get stuck and need some extra support at times...

How to Use

The Art of Transition

There are several different approaches to utilizing
The Art of Transition processing workbook

1

Individual

Go through the entire process from the beginning of the book on your own or with a personalized transition coach.

You may also choose to utilize tools per category: Unstuck, Movement or Transition processing.

2

Workshop

Attend The Art of Transition weeklong retreat or virtual workshop: Check TheWayBetween.org for current offerings

3

2-Day Life Plan

The workbook corresponds with the 2-day group discernment life plan. Having the first 4 sections filled out ahead of time aides in the process.

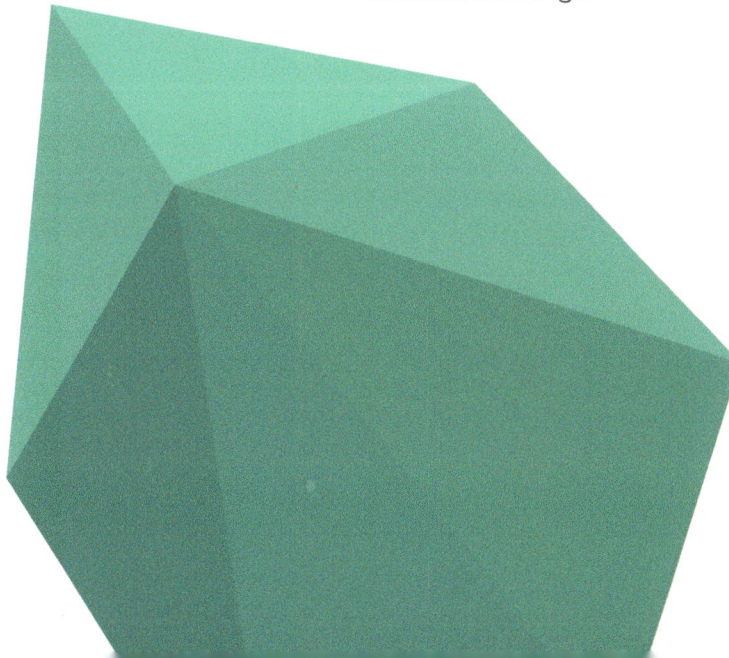

Contents
ARRANGED BY TOOL

🏃 MOVEMENT TOOLS

1

UNSTUCK TOOLS

TRANSITION TOOLS

FeedBack

Friend or Colleague Feedback Form

Your friend or colleague _____ has asked for your contribution to this process because you know her/him well enough to make accurate, wise, and discerning observations. Your direct, truthful feedback is a valuable contribution to his/her future decision-making. You are being invited to express any wonderments and/or questions you have had concerning your colleague's "fit" with his/her present roles, responsibilities, and direction of calling. In addition to vocational fit, please consider other angles of your friend's life including: Self care, financial stability, emotional support, family life and personal habits.

1. What is your relationship to the person who has asked you to participate in this discernment process?

2. What type of work appears to be most fulfilling for her/him?

3. What has been the best vocational role fit for your colleague so far?

4. Has s/he had any roles or responsibilities that have given you indication that s/he is in (or moving toward) a calling "sweet spot"?

5. What are her/his greatest strengths? (List at least 3)

6. What area of vocational responsibilities seem to be the most draining for your colleague? (Please explain)

7. What are her/his most challenging limitations in life or work? (List at least 3)

8. How are your colleague's strengths, natural abilities, and personality type contributing to their present role(s) and responsibilities in their vocation?

9. What do you see as developmental "edges" or areas the person needs to grapple with in some way in order to move forward?

We do not know who might find shelter in the things that we have made. We should see this as a liberating reality. It allows us to approach our craft with humility. This is a sacred task.

—Alabaster Co.

Creativity is God's gift to us.
Using our creativity is our
gift back to God.

— Christine Valters Paintner

Creativity flourishes when we have a sense of safety and self-acceptance.

— Julie Cameron

One day you will arrive, and
when you arrive you will need
to decide what story you will tell
about how you got there…and
when you get there, remember
that you were carried by the
Spirit. Hallelujah. Amen.
          —Alabaster Co.

The Way Between — thewaybetween.org

Facebook — @thewaybetween
Instagram — @waybetween
#thewaybetween

THE **WAY**
BETWEEN

About the Author

Sara takes the chaos out of transition! Utilizing whole brain engagement while strategically planning, is her unique contribution to life-planning and leadership development work! She has been creating and experimenting with multi-modal approaches to navigating major life transitions including creating The Art of Transition retreat experience, workbook and book (coming soon). She has worked as a cross-cultural transition coach with workers in more than 40 non-profit organizations over the last two decades. Sara holds a BA in Psychology, MA in Intercultural Studies and an ACC with the ICF (International Coaching Federation). She has served over 20 years in faith-based non-profit work, and in cross-cultural settings in Europe for 10 of those years. She now resides with her two children and husband in Denver, Colorado.

"Transition is a grand pause inviting us to discover once again if we are living into our unique purpose the great Creator designed us for. "

- How do we approach transition—especially difficult and often unwanted transitions—with our whole selves, not just our often spinning and frantic "mind"?
- How do we fully engage, embrace and receive from this unique season what is vital to learn?

The Art of Transition guides you through strategic processing, utilizing both logic (left-brain engagement) exercises, and creative brain integration (right-brain engagement) through simple but effective art and movement exercises.

This whole- person integrated approach is not only unique, but it is based in solid research and helps give relief to the all-to-familiar ruts of heavy cognitive processing we find ourselves in during the stress of transition, that bring with it anxiety and such limited awareness.

Through 6 main themes of transition, utilizing more than 35 holistic process tools— Movement tools, getting Unstuck tools, and Transition tools—you will find yourself with ample resources for creatively navigating your transition season! This resource guide can be utilized individually as a self-guided practice, or as a companion to the Art of Transition workshop experience, or 2-Day Life Planning process with your transition coach (see offerings at thewaybetween.org).

Praise for The Art of Transition:

"This was excellent! The content and process were well thought out and delivered. I am inspired to continue to use movement and right-brain activities in my own processing."
—Cross-cultural worker

"Experiencing the Art of Transition stretched my thinking and opened me up to new ways of interacting with God... for my everyday life, not just in transition."
—J.V. (Cross-cultural worker)

"I had been having panic attacks regularly after my recent transition. This workshop allowed me to be able to breath, attend to my body and do simple art techniques. Overall it grounded me in a way I didn't know I needed."
—J.T. (Cross-cultural worker)

"I want to make this a mandatory transition workshop for every worker in transition in our organization."
— V.T. (Cross-cultural regional leader)